IMAGES
of America

HOUSTON'S SPORTING LIFE 1900–1950

C. W. Bocock Jr. and E. L. Bringhurst pose for a studio shot in Houston baseball uniforms. It is easy to imagine that young Bocock had a fun and active home life. His father raised competition poultry around this time, and the Wyandottes and Leghorns must have made tempting targets for these boys. (Robert P. Cochran.)

ON THE COVER: A group of men poses in front of C. L. and Theo Bering's Hardware Store in downtown Houston. The huge stringer of bass and crappie likely came from one of hundreds of popular spots along area rivers and creeks, which were the places to freshwater fish in the days before Lake Houston or Lake Conroe were even considered. (Houston Metropolitan Research Center, Houston Public Library.)

IMAGES
of America

HOUSTON'S
SPORTING LIFE
1900–1950

Mike Vance

ARCADIA
PUBLISHING

Published by Arcadia Publishing
Charleston, South Carolina

Printed in the United States of America

Library of Congress Control Number: 2010938469

For all general information, please contact Arcadia Publishing:
Telephone 843-853-2070
Fax 843-853-0044
E-mail sales@arcadiapublishing.com
For customer service and orders:
Toll-Free 1-888-313-2665

Visit us on the Internet at www.arcadiapublishing.com

This book is dedicated to Dawson Vance, Tony Magdalena, and Jane Callaway for nurturing my lifelong love of sports and history.

CONTENTS

ACKNOWLEDGMENTS

Three of the top archives in Texas have been especially helpful in the preparation of this book: the Houston Metropolitan Research Center at the Houston Public Library (HMRC); the Woodson Research Center at the Fondren Library at Rice University (WRC); and the George Fuermann "Texas and Houston" Collection, 1836–2001, courtesy of special collections at the University of Houston Libraries (UHSC). I would like to thank Joel, Kemo, Aaron, Mary, Erin, Barbara, Tim, Liz, Laney, Marguerite, and Jo at HMRC; Lauren, Dara, and Amanda at WRC; and Nicci Westbrook at UHSC. Photographs without credits are part of the author's collection.

In no particular order, thanks go to researchers Bianca Vance, Alyssa Honnette and Sarah Conlon; Tom Kennedy for taking great pleasure in a few of the rabbit hunts; Story Sloane III for incredible images from his gallery; and Frances Trimble for help on Texas golf history. From country clubs in the area, thanks go to Gwen Elford at BraeBurn, Anna Lyons at Golfcrest, Van Barry and Mel Samuelson at River Oaks, and Sam Akkerman for help with the Houston Yacht Club. Thanks to Jill Brooks and Suzanne Graska for spreading the word; Jerry Brooks for photographs and golf conversation; Mary Vargo, Kirk Farris, and Bill McCurdy for answering more than a few questions about the East End, railroads, and baseball; and Mark Harrison and Everett Anschutz for consideration with Playland Park racing. Referrals came from Anne Sloan and Moises Villalpando. Thanks also goes to Ann Becker for actively helping in the hunt for photographs; Bill Bremer and Pat Schwab; Dena Houchin and Joan Miller from Dr. Denton Cooley's office; Angela McLeaf, Janice Sniker, Travis Davis, and Rusty Bloxom at the Battleship Texas; Walter and Cousin Cindy Carter; Miriam Morris Trost for providing access to her father's wonderful collection; Jack Waters, David Buckner, Laura Buckner, and "Matt" Matrisciani for help with Southern Pacific; Michael Botson for Hughes Tool; Susan and Mary Ellen Arbuckle and Bill Silva for help with the Arbuckle family; Valerie Boesch for gracious help with Houston Wrestling; Doug McLeod and Joe Kent for help with Galveston Bay fishing history; and Rowena Verdin, the charming librarian at Milby.

INTRODUCTION

From the state's first high school football champs to one of the nation's first Little League World Series winners, Houston has been home to more sports successes than residents might realize, even if the city's professional teams of the last half century have sometimes left a lackluster legacy.

The type of can-do attitude possessed by so many of the first Houstonians often brought with it a penchant for sporting. Journals from the days around the city's founding in 1836 talk about horse races held south of the few dirt streets that passed for the capitol city of Texas. Fast stock was prized, bragged over, and betted upon with frequency. When the horses didn't suffice, the gambling sort raced goats or pitted some of Houston's abundant rats against one another.

Baseball made an appearance in Houston before the Civil War, and a much-ballyhooed game between Houston and Galveston was played on the San Jacinto Battleground soon after the war. Though Galveston might have been the more cosmopolitan and influential city at the time, the Houston nine sent the Islanders home with tucked tails.

By 1900, diversion could be found in team sports played at every school in both city and suburb. The 50-year period covered by this book began with only 2 high schools in the city limits and ended with 10, rigidly segregated into 7 for whites and 3 for African Americans.

Companies competed with one another in baseball, basketball, and football in a variety of city recreational leagues. Boxing gyms, billiard halls, bowling alleys, and indoor shooting galleries were scattered around the area, several owned by German immigrants on main roads leading west or east of town, sometimes combined with beer gardens.

As the 20th century progressed, college sports sprang up as popular pastimes. Long before the American Football League's Oilers hit town, crowds packed a stadium on South Main Street to see the Rice Owls play against Southwest Conference foes. Baseball might have been the national pastime, but Rice University football games were major events in the Bayou City.

In the 1910s, the Houston College for Negroes played baseball and football, and three decades later, the new Texas Southern fielded teams. The University of Houston grew out of a Houston Independent School District junior college to become the metropolitan area's largest institution of higher learning, bringing sports teams with it along the way.

The Houston Buffs, the city's entry in the Texas League, was all the professional baseball Houstonians needed in the days when the major leagues came no closer to Texas than St. Louis. Fans crowded into West End Park in the first part of the century, then the new Buff Stadium, built along the interurban tracks to Galveston. The team was a Cardinal farm club for most of its existence, and Houston was filled with locals who rooted for the players they had cheered in Houston even after they moved on to St. Louis and the majors. For African American patrons in those days of segregation, the Houston Black Buffaloes incited the same passions.

Houston Wrestling at the City Auditorium was a thriving concern in the 1940s. Promoter Morris Siegel brought in the biggest wrestling crowds in the state to see big names, including former heavyweight boxing champ Primo Carnera and Gorgeous George, the star of the budding medium of television. Gorgeous George Wagner, by the way, was a Milby High School dropout.

Hunting and fishing have always been huge in southeast Texas. Waterfowl abounded all around the area. Deer were plentiful in woods that now hold neighborhoods, and freshwater and saltwater fish were to be found after an easy drive from downtown.

There was auto racing, drag racing, and air racing, volleyball, swimming, croquet, and even hockey. With no televisions or computer games, people went outside and played. The City of Houston established City Park, or Sam Houston Park, at the dawn of the 1900s, and new parks quickly followed in all sections of the city, filling a loud cry for more recreational opportunities.

There are several specific people who should be included in any discussion of Houston's sports history before 1950 but are not seen here for various reasons. Some of them grew to be among the city's most celebrated citizens. Before he was one of America's top defense attorneys, Richard "Racehorse" Haynes was lettering in track and football at Reagan High School. His famous nickname came not from the courtroom but from a coach who said he "ran like a racehorse." The world record black marlin, at 1,560 pounds, was caught by Houston oilman Alfred Glassell.

Others were best known for their athletic prowess itself. Slater Martin set city scoring records on the basketball court at Davis High School, led the Texas Longhorns to the Final Four, and went on to an NBA Hall of Fame career. Georgia Coleman, who learned to dive at the Heights Natatorium, moved to California and represented the United States in two Olympics, winning four medals and becoming the most celebrated woman diver of her day until she died at the tragically young age of 28.

Regrettably, authors are not always able to include photographs of every person who was on a wish list. Some photographs proved very difficult to find with sufficient quality, while others were privately held and rights couldn't be obtained.

The biggest disappointment is that no good images from the storied Yates-Wheatley football games of the 1940s came to the forefront. Held on Thanksgiving night, the contest was both the sporting and social event of the year in African American Houston, with fans crowding the Houston Independent School District stadium dressed to the nines. Yearbooks and school photographs from the segregated African American high schools, if any still exist, are sadly much less common than those from San Jacinto or Lamar, where the economic realities of the times allowed more students to afford luxuries like cameras and yearbooks.

It would take a very large volume to tell the comprehensive story of Houston sports during this 50-year span, and even then, it is a given that someone would be inadvertently overlooked. What is included here is a balanced overview of the types of activities in which Houstonians engaged whether as participants or as spectators. Houston is a great sports town today, at least partially thanks to this legacy passed down from earlier generations.

One

PROS AND COLLEGE

A Houston Buffs batter fouls one off at West End Park in 1910. The team had gone through a handful of monikers, including the "Babies," before settling on "Buffaloes." The ballpark suffered severe damage in the Hurricane of 1915. (Sloane Collection.)

The Houston Buffs of 1913 took the Texas League pennant for the fourth time in the club's history, repeating as champions from the year before. They specialized in aggressive base running from players like Pat Newnam and Red Davis. Pitching stars were Charles Rose, Dode Criss, and Andy Ware, whose pitching hand had been maimed in a childhood accident. (Houston Sports Museum/Finger Furniture.)

The precise orientation of the field at West End Park has been the subject of much discussion among modern-day historians, since the street grid that surrounded it was wiped away by construction of the "Pierce Elevated section" of Interstate 45. The uncovered stands down the third-base line appear to be segregated for use by African American fans at this early 1900s game. (HMRC.)

Opened in 1928, Buffalo Stadium sat on the west side of St. Bernard Street and the interurban line, now home to Finger Furniture at Cullen Boulevard and the Gulf Freeway. A crowd of 12,000 attended the opening game against the Waco Cubs. Around the top of the park are 80 medallions bearing a buffalo silhouette. (Mary Bavouset.)

The 1933 Buffs finished the regular season in first place but lost three straight to fourth-place San Antonio under a newly instituted playoff plan. Team president Fred Ankenman stands on the far left; he was working for the St. Louis Cardinals, who owned the franchise as a farm team of the big-league ball club. (Houston Sports Museum/Finger Furniture.)

The 1931 Houston Buffs claimed two future Hall of Famers in Dizzy Dean and Joe "Ducky" Medwick. In addition to Dean, the club had two other 20-game winners in George Washington Payne and Tex Carlton. The Buffs won the Texas League title with a sparkling record of 108-51. One mascot is the manager's son. Not much is known about the other mascot, Fritz (front right). (Houston Sports Museum/Finger Furniture.)

Jay Hanna "Dizzy" Dean pitched parts of the 1930 and 1931 seasons with the Buffs. In 1931, he went 26-10, struck out 303 batters in 304 innings, and posted an ERA of 1.53. All three marks topped the entire minor leagues. He also posted 11 shutouts—a Texas League record. Dean married a Houston woman that season in a ceremony at Buffs Stadium. (Houston Sports Museum/Finger Furniture.)

Allen Russell rose from a Houston Buffs parking lot attendant in the 1930s to become team president in the post-war years of 1946 to 1953. Russell was a master of promotion, and the Buffs outdrew the major-league St. Louis Browns in 1951. He also introduced amenities such as baseball's first air-conditioned ladies restroom. (Houston Sports Museum/Finger Furniture.)

With the 1950 season headed straight downhill, Houston Buffs club president Allen Russell came up with a "beat the heat" promotion, putting the local Double-A players in short, blousy pants. Russell was counting on curiosity to pump up gate receipts. He also thought it might increase interest among female fans. Players, not surprisingly, hated the idea, and when attendance dropped back to normal after a few weeks, long pants returned. (Sloane Collection.)

13

Grandma Brown was one, if not the best-known, fan of the Houston Buffaloes in the 1930s and 1940s. She was present at almost every home game, and most of the players knew her by name. Occasionally home games weren't enough, such as in this photograph commemorating a road trip she made to see the team play in Beaumont. (Houston Sports Museum/ Finger Furniture.)

Like minor-league baseball teams everywhere, the Houston Buffs of the Texas League relied on a variety of promotions to bring fans to the stadium. A lucky young man gets a new Schwinn bicycle as, from left to right, newsman Morris Frank, advertising man Roy Hofheinz, and the Buffs' Jerry Witte look on. Less than 10 years later, Hofheinz was part of a group trying to bring Major League Baseball to Houston. (Houston Sports Museum/Finger Furniture.)

The Buffs appear to have given up a run late in the 1910 season. Atop the stands is an early sign of one of the biggest sporting events of the year in Houston. Tulane and Texas A&M University played football at West End Park on Thanksgiving Day that year with the Aggies winning 17-0. Neutral sites were popular for big football games, since travel was sometimes challenging. The University of Texas playing A&M at West End Park on a November Monday was a brief Houston tradition of the day. (Sloane Collection.)

During World War I, patriotism and duty were found everywhere in the country, and Rice Institute was no exception. Ninety percent of the male students and half the faculty were enlisted into a military lifestyle complete with uniforms, daily drills, and reveille at dawn. When the Rice Owls journeyed to play Texas in 1917, the student body turned out en masse and marched through downtown Austin. Students hated the loss of "trips to Blodgett for foaming tankards." (WRC.)

The offensive stars were Leroy Bell, "Preacher" Lindsay, and Troy "Bullet" Sullivan as the Rice Owls won their first-ever game against Texas by the 13-0 score memorialized in this photograph. Bell, a transfer from Central State Normal in Edmund, Oklahoma, went over for the school's first-ever touchdown against the Longhorns when he put it across in the fourth quarter at Austin's Clark Field. (WRC.)

The Rice Owls beat the Arkansas Razorbacks by a score of 40-7 in this season-ending game played at the athletic field on South Main Street on November 27, 1919. Stars for the Owls were quarterback Paul Nash, who had recently returned from the U.S. Army, and left halfback Graves McGee, of Abilene. Coach Phil Arbuckle was a pioneer in splitting his guards and starting running backs from an athletic stance. (WRC.)

The 1919 Rice Institute football team huddles together on the sideline during a one-sided victory against Arkansas. The win would leave the team with an 8-1 record on the year, with the only blemish being a 32-7 loss to the Texas Longhorns in Austin. One of the victories was a triumph over Howard Payne University, earned when the Yellow Jackets' coach withdrew from the contest over what he considered a bad call. (WRC.)

The 1913 Rice Owls football team, playing in their second year of existence, went 4-0 on the season with only two of the wins coming against college competition. It opened against a military team, Signal Corps Company B, and then beat Houston High School 7-0 before finishing with wins over Southwestern University and Trinity University. Coach Phillip Arbuckle came to Houston from Southwestern in Georgetown, at times coaching baseball, basketball, and track, too. He had a winning football season every year at Rice until his final one in 1923, and he finished with the highest winning percentage in Owls football history. (WRC.)

Houston College moved from rented quarters to this campus of its own on San Felipe Road, today's West Dallas, in 1894. As was the case with many institutions, the football team of 1914 cobbled together what schedule it could, likely playing other African American colleges and high schools and perhaps a few industrial teams. The sole remnant of the school's campus lies in the name of College Memorial Park Cemetery. (HMRC.)

In the early years of Rice Institute, the athletic fields were located at the corner of South Main Street and University Boulevard. In the beginning, spectators stood to watch the action in baseball or football, but by 1926 stands graced both sides of the field, some affording views of the new Hermann Hospital. (WRC.)

Bob Brumley scores one of his three touchdowns against Baylor University in 1940. He also kicked three extra points to account for all 21 points Rice scored in the victory. In 1943, two years after leaving Rice, Brumley joined the staff of the U.S. Navy fitness program at Oklahoma University and played on the Sooners team at age 26 when he ran for eight touchdowns, passed for two, and caught one.

The 1940 Owls head to the gridiron at Rice Field. The old football horseshoe sat where the track and soccer stadium is today, near the corner of South Main Street and University Boulevard. It held about 37,000 people and was generally packed in the days when Rice football was the highest level of competition to be found in the Bayou City.

Jess Neely (third from the left), seen with his first Rice staff, was easily the winningest head coach in the school's football history. He came to the Owls from Clemson University in 1940 and stayed on Main Street until 1966. When he retired, he had taken Rice to seven bowl games, won four Southwest Conference championships, and was among the top-10 college coaches in all-time victories with 208.

Rice wingback Bob Perkins returns a punt against the University of Texas Longhorns in 1942. The Longhorns handed Rice its only Southwest Conference loss of the season. The Owls also had a scoreless tie with Texas A&M on their schedule, and as a result they finished a half-game behind Texas for the conference crown that year.

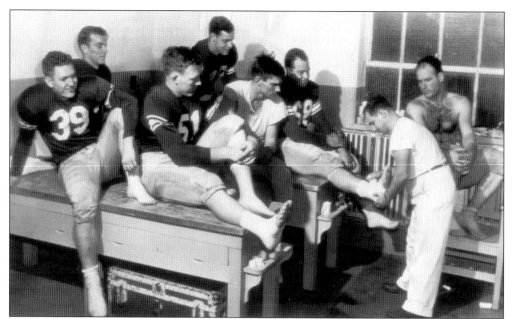

Rice trainer Eddie Wojecki tapes the ankle of guard J. W. Magee in a posed photograph taken on November 25, 1946, the day the Southwest Conference co-champion Owls learned they would be headed to the Orange Bowl in Miami to face the Tennessee Volunteers. Rice's defensive powerhouse held Tennessee to only five first downs for the entire contest, winning the game 8-0. (WRC.)

On the far right-hand side of this photograph, Cougars kicker Ken Hawkins is in the process of putting one through the uprights. The University of Houston was in the second of three seasons in the Lone Star Conference in 1947. It would join Trinity University, North Texas State, and Midwestern State University in 1949 to create the four-team Gulf Coast Conference before bolting for the Missouri Valley Conference in 1951.

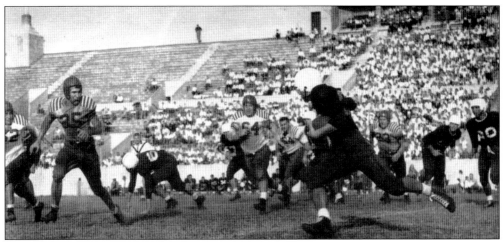

A white-helmeted runner gains yardage that would lead the Trinity Tigers to a 20-0 victory over the University of Houston. The Cougars played their home games in the stadium that was opened by the Houston Independent School District in 1941 at a time when the school district was still closely connected to the university. Six years later, the "Coogs" sometimes had difficulty filling up the stadium that is known today as Robertson Stadium.

Chester Ryan racks up some of his game-high yardage in the New Year's Day Classic of 1948. In the first year playing under its new identity of Texas State University for Negroes, the football team was the pride of the campus. The team went 8-3 that season, including a 12-0 win over rival Prairie View.

This photograph of a running back escaping is a bit of a metaphor for the University of Houston's 1947 football season. Athletic director Harry Fouke led the striped-shouldered Cougars into intercollegiate athletics only a season earlier. This campaign started with three straight victories over Centenary College, McMurry University, and Daniel Baker College, but those wins were followed by eight consecutive losses. Fouke remained athletic director at Houston until 1979 and oversaw much success for the Coogs.

For the Rice Owls, 1926–1927 was not a banner year in basketball. At 0-9, they were the only school in the Southwest Conference that failed to notch a win. They had only one conference win the previous season, in a game against Texas with Ralph Nevinger scoring all of the Owls' points in a disputed overtime period. For Rice coach Franklyn Ashcraft, it was the end of the line, proving that pressure to win is nothing new. (WRC.)

The Rice Owls were Southwest Conference co-champions in 1942–1943. As a reward for a great year, the Owls earned a postseason trip to Madison Square Garden, where they lost to the local five from St. John's by a score of 51-49. Co-captains Bill Closs and Hal Lambert, both All-Southwest Conference team members, were among five Owls who later played for the Houston Mavericks, the city's first professional team, which lasted only two games.

The first buildings at the University of Houston Central Campus were only one year old in 1940, and the basketball program that would spawn "Phi Slamma Jamma" some decades later would not take on intercollegiate competition until after World War II. Nonetheless, these players took the games seriously, competing and winning in the city recreational league. The young Cougars finished second in 1940–1941.

The women's basketball team at Texas State University for Negroes did not play a very full schedule in 1947 according to their yearbook, the *Tiger*. It was the first year the university existed under its new name thanks to an act by the Texas Legislature. Students and faculty, still trying to end segregation, were successful in getting the name changed to Texas Southern University in 1951.

The Rice yearbook, the *Campanile*, described tennis in the second decade of the century as "by far the most important sport among women." Organized in the spring of 1915, members of the Rice Girls' Tennis Club held tournaments throughout the school year with the grand finale of competition being held in conjunction with commencement exercises. (WRC.).

The University of Houston's men's tennis team won the Lone Star Conference title in 1947–1948. Glenn Hewitt (on the left, standing) won the singles title and combined with Jason Morton for the doubles crown as well. Morton (in the center, squatting) was the state singles champ in Texas as a senior at Lamar High School in 1946.

These young ladies, exercising on the tennis courts of Houston College for Negroes in 1914, made up a good portion of the student body of 109. The tidy campus was operated in part by the Baptist Missionary and Educational Association of Texas. Rev. Jack Yates was associated with the founding of the school in the 1880s. (HMRC.)

From left to right, Dick Morris, Jack Rodgers, Sid Nachlas, and Jimmy Whitehurst are pictured in 1941 as the Southwest Conference champion Rice Owls tennis team. Morris, who would win the prestigious Bob Quin Award that is given to the most outstanding senior male athlete at Rice, had recently come within two points of beating professional Bobby Riggs at the River Oaks Tournament.

Because the Rice Institute opened midway through 1912, missing baseball season, the first "nine" did not compete until the following year. By 1917, the Rice Owls team picture already shows a disparity in old and new uniforms, including one player who appears to be wearing a high school jersey. The team went 8-5-1 in the final year that Phillip Arbuckle coached baseball as well as football. (WRC.)

The star of the 1922 Rice baseball team was lefty Eddie Dyer (second from the left, front row), who signed with the St. Louis Cardinals following the Owls' season. Though an arm injury ended his professional pitching career, he served as a manager in the Cardinals system until 1950, including three straight first-place finishes for their Texas League affiliate Houston Buffs. Dyer's managerial high point was a World Series win over Boston in 1946. (WRC.)

The Houston Independent School District established separate junior colleges for whites and African Americans in 1927. Within eight years, it had more than 700 students and offered a four-year degree though classes were still held at night at Yates High School. The school's sports teams competed against high schools and other segregated institutions such as Wiley College in Marshall and Texas College in Tyler. (HMRC.)

Rice's track team of 1921 poses with the new $75,000 field house building in the background. Athletic director Phil Arbuckle (in the suit and tie) served as coach. "Preacher" Lindsay (back row, center) was the star sprinter and team captain. The team won multiple meets and finished second in the Southwest Conference championships held that year at Waco. (WRC.)

The mile relay team at Rice in 1927 poses with coach Ernie Hjertberg, who had won the championship of the U.S. Track Association in the two-mile steeplechase twice, in 1891 and 1892. Before coming to Rice, Hjertberg was a highly praised coach at the New York Athletic Club, the Irish American Athletic Club, and for the Swedish National Track Team. (WRC.)

Coach Archie French led the University of Houston hockey club in 1940. The team performed well and took eventual league champion Rice to a decisive two-game playoff round at the end of the year. The Coogs took the first game, but the Owls beat them in the second one by a high enough margin to prevail on cumulative points and win the title.

Rice hockey in 1940 was an independent outfit that relied on financial support from outside the university offices. They played games against schools, clubs, and even trounced a team from the U.S. Army's Camp Wallace 11-3. The crowd that showed up to watch the team's victory over the University of Houston in the season championship finale was the largest ever to see hockey in Houston up to that time.

The University of Houston Foil Club competed with other colleges and universities around the state of Texas, plus other opponents as far ranging as the fencing clubs of Houston and Dallas and the Carbide Buccaneers. Twenty-five years later, Claude Caux, a fencing master and mime instructor, arrived at the University of Houston campus where he instructed almost a generation of students in fencing and stage combat.

Channel 2 went on the air as KLEE with lots of time that had to be filled with local programming. The station began broadcasting baseball and football games almost from the start. Stadiums of the day were not built with special camera locations, and camera operators like Gorman Erickson were often in the midst of the fans. The Hobby family bought the station in June 1950, changing the call letters to KPRC. (Bill Bremer.)

Two

TEAM SPORTS

Industrial leagues were enormously popular among Houston sports fans. Even those who did not play often came out to watch these games. It was also common practice for industrial league teams to play Houston high schools in baseball and basketball. (HMRC.)

Phillip Arbuckle, athletic director at Rice Institute, was also de facto athletic director at Camp Logan. His uniform is likely a product of the widespread Reserve Officers Training Corps (ROTC) approach taken on the Rice campus. In the summer of 1918, with Rice out of session, Arbuckle coached the main Camp Logan baseball team in the municipal league against competitors that included Ellington Field and Universal Shipyards. (Susan Arbuckle.)

The tens of thousands of soldiers training at Camp Logan in the West End, most from the Illinois National Guard, were looking for diversion. Sports activities of all sorts were popular at Camp Logan throughout the 20 months that it was filled with troops. The well-equipped medical unit team was one of dozens of baseball teams at the camp. (HMRC.)

The Houston Lighting and Power Company was the dynasty of its day in Houston City League baseball. The city's businesses competed in an oil league and an industrial league, and results were covered in the newspapers, all the way down to the anticipated return of a player-employee named Bruce Bellflower who had missed four games with a "lame foot." (HMRC.)

Men's baseball in the city leagues was incredibly popular during the first half of the 20th century. Businesses were known to recruit employees for their hitting or pitching prowess. Softball was also played by the 1940s and 1950s, but it was fast-pitch—not the case today. (Miriam Trost, William A. Morris Collection.)

The baseball team for Levy's Department Store poses atop its building at Main and Walker Streets. Amateur baseball was enormously popular throughout the first half of the 20th century. A Houston City League had been formed in 1911, and the parks and recreation department began organizing play in 1924. (HMRC.)

The Southern Pacific Railroad, the city's largest employer, fielded a baseball team for its African American workers. This 1926 edition lost the city championship of the segregated league to the Monarchs 9-8. Among other teams in that circuit were the Lincoln Theatre Stars, who represented Houston's largest African American movie house, which was owned by local NAACP leader O. P. DeWalt. (Frank J. Liuzza.)

John and James Liuzza, brothers who owned a grocery business in the Fifth Ward, established the Houston Monarchs, an African American baseball team, in the early 1920s. They built this ballpark near Cline and Grove Streets across from their other businesses. A few years later, the Liuzzas opened Monarch Stadium on Gillespie Street nearby. (Frank J. Liuzza.)

The Houston Monarchs operated as an amateur and semi-professional baseball team during the 1920s and 1930s, going against competition fielded by both white and African American team owners. The identities of these players have not been discovered, but among them are pitcher "Lightning" Rodgers and catcher "Noisy" Tillman. (Frank J. Liuzza.)

Ellington Field's football coach, L. H. Bankart, was an All-American end in 1909 and brought coaching experience from Colgate University and Dartmouth College. Almost all of his players were college lettermen, too. The airfield's yearbook stated, "Little importance has been attached to developing football and baseball teams. These were chosen at random for only one purpose—'to keep Camp Logan in its place.' " Ellington beat Camp Logan 3-0

Hughes Tool's 1930 football team won the championship among Houston's amateur teams. The coach was Jimmy Delmar (in the sweater and tie), who came to Hughes Tool as athletic director with a background as a prizefighter and gym owner. He also coached the baseball team at Grand Prize Brewery, a subsidiary of Hughes Tool Company, in the 1930s. Delmar went on to serve on the Houston School Board as part of the anti-communist slate in the 1950s. Delmar Stadium complex bears his name. (HMRC.)

uss Texas. *1923*

The USS *Texas* was part of the U.S. Navy's Pacific Fleet in 1923 and took time in port to complete its football schedule against the other U.S. battleships in that part of the world. Between a variety of maneuvers and goodwill trips, the games were fitted in during the fall football season and played on the naval base gridiron. The team was outfitted in state-of-the-art uniforms and pads. The ship's newspaper documents highly anticipated contests against the *Wyoming*, *New York*, and *Arkansas*. (Battleship Texas.)

Southern Pacific Railroad opened its new track and athletic field on Oliver Street, north of Washington Avenue, in 1924. It is located roughly where Target sits off Interstate 10. Each May, the field was packed with employees representing shop, terminal, and office workers from Houston and men and women from the divisions in San Antonio, Austin, Dallas, Lafayette, El Paso, and Beaumont, which was the winningest team in the late 1920s. The band was also made up of Southern Pacific workers. (HMRC.)

The annual track competition among the fleetest workers of Houston's largest employer, Southern Pacific Railroad, was fierce. The winners of the Houston division then faced those from the railroad's New Orleans division. Medals and trophies were on the line in junior, senior, and girls division. Not surprisingly, any travel required was via the Southern Pacific terminal. (HMRC.)

Women were not left out of the track competition entirely, though they were offered only two events: a 220-yard relay and a 75-yard dash. They were encouraged to compete against other "girls" in softball and other sports. The weekend also featured special trains to Galveston and a Southern Pacific Day at Luna Park. (HMRC.)

As the signs indicate—though the track meet was the headliner of the annual weekend of competition among employees—there was also a team golf competition at Hermann Park, as well as baseball, boxing, bowling, trap and pistol shooting, and horseshoes. The large Saturday night dance was held at City Auditorium. (HMRC.)

Race fans flocked to Epsom Downs north of town on Humble Road by train and automobile to watch the ponies run. By the time the second meet opened in March 1934, the stables had

Texas legalized pari-mutuel gambling on horse racing at the height of the Great Depression, and Epsom Downs opened on Thanksgiving Day 1933 to a crowd of about 27,000—the largest sporting crowd in Houston history up to that time. The track also employed more than 400 people every race day and put hundreds of thousands of dollars into the state coffers. In spite of the success, the state repealed gambling, and the track closed early in 1937.

been expanded to provide housing for 1,000 horses, most of which were brought in by train from California and Florida to race the Texas meets. (HMRC.)

Racing publications around the country lauded Epsom Downs as being up-to-date in every way. The opening meets from late November through mid-December in 1933 drew extra attention, since most other American horse tracks were idle at the time. The track cost well more than $500,000 to construct and contained a "totalizer," a state-of-the-art way to record mutuel wagers. Winning horses fared well, too, with track owners reporting purses of about $140,000 per meet. Spectators paid a $1 admission to the grandstands, a good thing since the track went through 20 tons of hay daily and reported an expenditure of $13,500 in 1934 for carrots alone. (HMRC.)

The 1940 girls' riding club at Austin High School was called the Mustang Mounties and had one stated goal—good horsemanship. Rules were that each girl must go horseback riding at least twice every six weeks. They were also required to take an active role in the social life of the club according to sponsor Mrs. E. C. Gates. The City of Houston provided bridle paths at Hermann, MacGregor, and Memorial Parks.

The popular riding club at the University of Houston was called the Buckaroos, and it had a busy year in 1940–1941. In addition to campus activities such as a December hayride and weiner roast, members rode downtown in the annual Fat Stock Show Parade and made trips to ride in Austin and Bandera.

The USS *Texas* squad was the fleet basketball champion earlier in the 1920s while stationed in the Pacific. By the end of the decade, the vessel was based at the New York Navy Yard and was seeing regular duty as part of the scouting fleet. The *Texas*'s basketball team doesn't look like an above-the-rim–type squad, but it competed gamely in a league made up of the other Atlantic battleships such as the *Utah* and *Arkansas*. (Battleship Texas.)

In 1930, the Hughes Tool Company employed about 2,000 people, including 450 African Americans. For the white employees, the company maintained an athletic complex at the northeast corner of the Hughes Tool complex located southeast of downtown. They fielded teams in all sorts of sports, including men's volleyball. (HMRC.)

Owning a summerhouse at Morgan's Point on Galveston Bay was popular among well-to-do Houstonians who enjoyed recreation in the outdoors. In addition to warm weather water sports, activities such as shuffleboard made for a nice winter diversion at the home of Judge Sam Streetman's family on Bay Ridge Road. Streetman had been a county judge in Milam County before moving to Houston for even greater legal prominence. (Houston Yacht Club Archives, Streetman Collection.)

Much like the Astrodome in later decades, Buff Stadium was used for so much more than just Houston Buffs baseball games. High school football was a staple, and the circus was held in the parking lot every year. Here workers set up the track for a televised roller derby in 1949. (Bill Bremer.)

Three
INDIVIDUAL SPORTS

From the early days of American golf, the sport carried great appeal for well-to-do women. The Women's Texas Golf Association formed in 1916, and its second state amateur championship tournament was held at Houston Country Club in late April 1917. Sixty-nine women showed up on qualifying day, with 56 advancing to four days of match play. San Antonio's Edna Lapham won, which was part of a five-year run as champion. (HMRC.)

The first golf club in Houston was organized in 1904, when local businessmen leased a 56-acre tract on the south bank of Buffalo Bayou and built a course and a $5,000 clubhouse. Many of the 110 charter members are posing here in February 1906 with star golfers who staged an exhibition. Among those who wowed the locals with their talent on the links were Andrew Kirkaldy, George Low, Rolland Jones, Alex Finley, and former British Open champion Sandy Herd. (UHSC.)

In 1908, members from the four-year-old Houston Golf Club bought their own land on the southeast outskirts of town and formed the Houston Country Club. Early members included the city's elite, such as Jesse Jones, H. Baldwin Rice, William Ward Watkin, Abe Levy, and John Henry Kirby. The grounds included a pool and tennis courts, and the clubhouse facilities included a full kitchen and a few apartments.

Golf legend Walter Hagen makes a putt in front of a large gallery during an exhibition at River Oaks Country Club. By this time, Hagen had won most of his 11 major championships and was earning more than $100,000 a year. One story has it that Hagen's limousine stopped to pick up a young man who was hitchhiking to the event at River Oaks Country Club, and Hagen let him work as his caddy. (Sloane Collection.)

Smiling for the camera instead of watching the flight of a golf ball, this is a glamour shot designed to sell cutting-edge golf attire. Though men had been wearing knickers or plus fours since the end of the Civil War, early female golfers wore long skirts and jackets. A typical golf bag for either sex contained only four or five wood-shafted clubs. (HMRC.)

Houston native Jimmy Demaret discovered golf as a caddy for soldiers at Camp Logan. He won the city caddy tournament in 1923 at the age of 12. Demaret became caddy master at Hermann Park Golf Course, then River Oaks Country Club, and served as head professional at Galveston Municipal Golf Course and BraeBurn Country Club. While in Galveston, he briefly considered trying a career as a professional singer, but nightclub owner Sam Maceo gave him money to stick with golf. (BraeBurn Country Club.)

Hermann Park Golf Course opened in July 1923 with city officials playing a one-hole match with gold-colored golf balls supplied by sporting goods merchant C. L. Bering. It was the first public course in the city of Houston. Players enjoyed real grass greens as opposed to sand putting surfaces that were common in some municipal settings around the country. (HMRC.)

From left to right, Byron Nelson, Jimmy Demaret, and Jack Burke Sr. take a break during the week of the 1940 Western Open played at River Oaks Country Club where Burke was the golf professional. Demaret, then the head professional at BraeBurn, won the event, taking the title from Nelson. During his 1936–1941 tenure at BraeBurn Country Club, Demaret won eight PGA events, including the 1940 Masters. (River Oaks Country Club.)

Colonial Country Club was foreclosed upon after only a few years of existence. A group bought the 18-hole golf course on Richmond Road for $60,000 in 1931 and reorganized it as BraeBurn Country Club. The course, designed by John Bredemus, was built on 165 acres along Brays Bayou where it took in Keegans Bayou. (BraeBurn Country Club.)

During World War II, production of golf balls was greatly curtailed due to rubber shortages, and many courses let grass overgrow sand traps or they closed all together. Houston, with its busy industries, fared better. Locals paid $1 each to watch a Thursday afternoon match for war relief that brought, from left to right, Johnny Weissmuller, Bob Hope, Jimmy Demaret, Byron Nelson, and Bing Crosby to BraeBurn County Club. The Red Cross was behind the mid-February 1942 tour that brought Hollywood celebrities and golf stars together. The trio of movie stars also made stops in Dallas and San Antonio, with Houston being the middle leg of their jaunt through Texas. Ben Hogan had been part of the Dallas event but skipped Houston and went to San Antonio to play the Texas Open, losing the tourney in an 18-hole playoff. (BraeBurn Country Club.)

Tennis was a popular sport at Houston parks in the decades prior to World War II. City parks offering free tennis courts in the 1930s and 1940s included Cherryhurst, Eastwood, MacGregor, Mason, Memorial, Milroy, and Settegast. (Miriam Trost, William A. Morris Collection.)

The *Houston Post* wrote of bowling on March 26, 1899 that "interest in the pastime is on the increase." Passion was especially high among the area's German citizens. The Turnverein, which competed in the sport against German clubs in Dallas and Galveston, added eight additional alleys to its building in 1903. There were two bowling and beer garden facilities out the Harrisburg Road. (HMRC.)

After earning his living as a lifeguard with occasional games of basketball for pay, Paul Boesch had his first professional wrestling match in 1932. Over the next 10 years, he wrestled as a contender around the United States, Canada, Australia, Japan, and the Philippines. (Valerie Boesch.)

Paul Boesch returned from army service in World War II as a highly decorated veteran with medals that included a Silver Star, Bronze Star, Purple Heart, and French Croix de Guerre. After a 1947 car accident virtually ended his career inside the ring, Boesch joined Houston Wrestling promoter Morris Sigel as a radio and then television announcer, eventually becoming the promoter himself. (Valerie Boesch.)

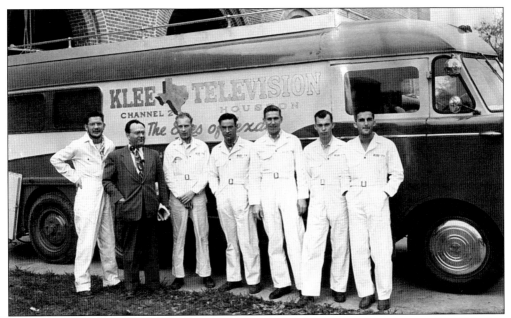

KLEE, the first television station in southeast Texas, developed a sports presence right off the bat when it opened in 1949. The entire remote broadcast crew, complete with matching coveralls, poses here prior to one of the weekly Friday night wrestling shows at City Auditorium. The popular hour-long program often ran several minutes long until promoter Morris Sigel schooled wrestlers to miraculously finish the bouts in time for the evening news. (Bill Bremer.)

W. Keating operated this pool hall at 414 Travis Street and also rented out rooms to a collection of lodgers. The hall was an all-male environment complete with spittoons and signs on the wall reminding players not to place any marks on the billiard balls. In the first decade of the century, it competed with Main Street billiard establishments like the Cabinet, which also offered an oyster parlor, and Coney Island, which included a bowling alley. (HMRC.)

Galveston native Jack Johnson was a polarizing figure in the rigidly segregated world during his reign as heavyweight champ from 1908 to 1915. Among his many troubles with the law, Johnson was jailed for 24 days for prizefighting in Galveston at a time when the sport was illegal in Texas. African Americans loved to see him toy with white opponents, and Houston newspapers told of trouble between spectators gathered to watch live updates posted on the side of the Houston Chronicle Building. (Chicago Historical Society.)

Boxers prepare to meet in a wooden ring for a bout sponsored by the YMCA at Ellington Field in 1918. The YMCA had two buildings to enhance life at the base, providing pianos, phonographs and records, religious services, and athletic events, with boxing being the most popular. The organization claimed, "Some of the best bouts in the South have been staged at Ellington under Y auspices."

Boxing matches took place among fellow crewman, but the big excitement was when competition could be arranged against other ships or navy yard personnel. In 1920, fighters from the USS *Texas* took part in bouts at San Pedro and Mare Island in California, at Bremerton, Washington, and in Panama. Often "smokers"—unregulated, informal boxing matches—were thrown together with fights hosted by a given ship or at a popular port bar. (Battleship Texas.)

With as many as 2,000 sailors and marines aboard the battleship USS *Texas*, entertainment was always welcome. Boxing among sailors was one of the sporting activities regularly enjoyed during wartime. The ship's newspaper stated that boxing was "as much a part of the Navy as mess gear or liberty blues." This bout took place in February 1945 toward the end of World War II and the end of the vessel's commission. (Battleship Texas.)

ONE MILE RACE ON BOARD THE TEXAS
THANKSGIVING DAY   VERA CRUZ MEX.
PHOTO BY CHARLAND

Harris County's treasured battleship USS *Texas* was commissioned at Newport News, Virginia, in March 1914 and shortly thereafter was dispatched to Mexican waters to help quell a breakdown in relations with that government. Her officers and crew celebrated Thanksgiving of that year at Veracruz with activities that included this relay race around the deck among the sailors. (Battleship Texas.)

Though it traveled the world protecting America in two wars, the USS *Texas* has been resting along the Houston Ship Channel since 1946. While a commissioned warship, its sailors competed with other U.S. Navy crews in every activity imaginable. Sailors also reveled in friendly competition among crewmates, even while underway. Wrestling was one of many options. (Battleship Texas.)

The Polar Wave Ice Skating Palace was an outgrowth of Polar Wave Ice and Fuel at 2203 McGowen Street, which was incorporated by Montrose addition founder J. W. Link, W. R. Eckhardt, and Elwyn Carrol in early 1922. It was one of many companies that supplied blocks of ice to go in Houstonians' iceboxes to cool their food. The giant ice rink was constructed around the corner a few years later. (HMRC.)

In addition to the regular hockey competition spawned by the introduction of the Polar Wave Ice Skating Palace into Houston's sporting venues, there was still plenty of plain, old-fashioned ice-skating; and wherever there are girls and boys, there will be boys showing off. These two high schoolers get an open lane to spray ice at the photographer. (Sloane Collection.)

Though the sign reads Ford Parts, the hood ornament is from a mid-1920s Chrysler. Many owners or drivers were tinkerers who assembled their own machines. These dirt track cars had only one seat. Road or endurance racing was also popular in the 1920s, but those cars often had two seats to provide for a mechanic. (Sloane Collection.)

A race car christened "Miss Houston" revs its engine at the Houston Speedway, located southwest of town. The straight pipes caused minimal back pressure from the exhaust but created a great deal of noise. (Sloane Collection.)

Cars careen around the track at Arrowhead Speedway near Old Spanish Trail and Main Street in 1949. Certain top local drivers became legendary like Doc Cossey and Billy Griswold and, starting in 1953, a young man named A. J. Foyt. Across the prairie to the northwest is the backside of Glenn McCarthy's brand new Shamrock Hotel, which opened with national fanfare on St. Patrick's Day the year of this race. The photograph does a terrific job of orienting the location of Arrowhead Speedway. (Sloane Collection.)

Much like Playland Park, the track at Arrowhead Speedway was a tight one—the type of oval measuring less than one mile that today's NASCAR fans would equate to tracks at Bristol, Tennessee, or Martinsville, Virginia. The popularity among drivers can be seen by the high numbers hand painted on some cars and a handful that have no numbers at all. (Sloane Collection.)

Crowds of more than 2,000 people filled the grandstands at Playland Park Raceway every weekend, lured by the roar of the stock car engines and the smell of exhaust. As with most race fans, crashes made things exciting. The no. 114 car is in need of its sponsor's services. (Karen A. Anschutz/ Carolyn Thompson's Antiques of Texas.)

Playland Park had games, a miniature train, and rides like the Wild Mouse and the roller coaster seen beyond the fence at the racetrack. In pre-Astroworld days, the park off South Main Street was the place to go for high schoolers and families. (Karen A. Anschutz/Carolyn Thompson's Antiques of Texas.)

Auto racing became immensely popular in Houston almost as soon as there were cars. By mid-century, much of the action was centered near Main Street, south of town. (Karen A. Anschutz/ Carolyn Thompson's Antiques of Texas.)

Drivers at Playland Park in 1949 had no head and neck restraints or Nomex suits. The doors to the cars weren't even welded shut. These truly were stock cars, and though some drivers gained a following as local favorites, their racing equipment was often a high school football helmet and a lively sport shirt. (Karen A. Anschutz/Carolyn Thompson's Antiques of Texas.)

The stands, located close to the action at Playland Park, were protected by these low wooden fences at the beginning of the 1950s and by a taller metal one by the end of the decade. However, tragedy struck there on Saturday, September 5, 1959. The car driven by regular driver Blackie Lothringer left the track, flew over a fence, and killed three people at the edge of the parking lot near a concession stand. Not long after, racing came to an end at Playland Park. (Karen A. Anschutz/Carolyn Thompson's Antiques of Texas.)

Four

HIGH SCHOOLS

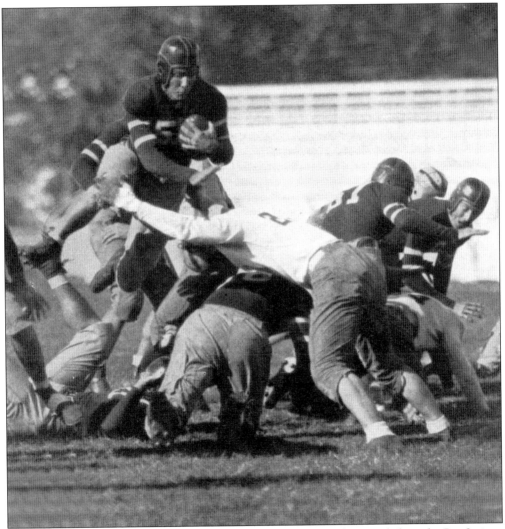

Wylie E. Summers took over as head football coach in 1933 and promptly brought San Jacinto High School its first city district championship. Summers was a graduate of San Marcos State Teacher's College, now known as Texas State University. He fielded a team of talented players, 10 of whom were named All-City.

Before starting the 1927 season, the football team from Sam Houston High School held a two-week training camp to prepare for the upcoming campaign. Thirty boys made the trip to Camp Ross Sterling, Jr., which had been opened at Cedar Point on Trinity Bay to honor the recently deceased son of the Humble Oil Founder and future Texas governor. The team's coach announced that the players focused on hard work and fundamentals.

Pat Quinn was a Central High School alumnus who returned to fill the need for a football coach in 1917, a year when high school boys were possibly thinking of other battles. Central High School, also known as "Sam Houston," was the only high school among city schools until Houston annexed the Heights that year. The "Orange and Black" returned only one letterman in 1918, with many boys entering the service.

The Houston skyline is visible from the sidelines of the football field at Jefferson Davis High School in 1931. The top of the bell tower at Holy Name Catholic Church also protrudes over the nearby building tops. With only five high schools in Houston, the Jefferson Davis team's schedule reached to include teams from surrounding cities. These Panthers went 4-5-1 playing teams from Bryan, Beaumont, Lufkin, Port Arthur, Goose Creek, and St. Thomas High School.

A variety of equipment could be found in local high school football in the mid- to late 1920s, though several of the players in this game are not even wearing helmets, something that was not unusual for the era. Rules requiring every football player to wear helmets didn't start until the 1930s. Likewise, spectators were allowed to line up right at the edge of the field, even bringing their cars.

Young Bussey won his first letter as a sophomore on the 1934 San Jacinto High School football team, but he also starred in basketball as one of two players to score more than 100 total points during that eight-game season. He went on to Louisiana State University and was drafted in 1940 by the Chicago Bears. After playing one NFL season, he entered the service. Bussey was killed in action in the Philippines in January 1945.

"Three yards and a cloud of dust" was an old saw that still applied to most high school football teams in 1927, though college coaches like Pop Warner were starting to utilize the forward pass more often. This San Jacinto Bears game was played at West End Park, normally the home of the Houston Buffs baseball team, but it was also a destination for big-time Houston high school football, as was Rice Field.

The University Interscholastic League began overseeing competition in certain high school sports throughout the state of Texas in 1920, and the winner of the first-ever state football championship were the Bulldogs of Houston Heights High School. Similar claims were made in the town of Cleburne, as well, since the final score of the contest was 0-0. (HMRC.)

Milam "Mike" Jones was an early star of Milby football, winning the Looney Trophy that was awarded to the most valuable player among the Buffaloes. Lettering three years at center, Jones was also the first Milby football player ever picked to play in the Texas North-South All-Star Game in his senior year of 1941. (Milby High School.)

The 1939 football squad at Stephen F. Austin High School was the first big winner in the short, three-year history of the program. They went 9-2-2 under coaches John Scott and Sam Lefkowitz. Harold Stockbridge was the star player who led the Mustangs. The only team losses came at the hands of McAllen High School and Waco High School.

A Reagan High School player, wearing maroon with the trademark white shoulders, is brought to the ground by a bevy of opposing players. One of the defenders is wearing a helmet with a face mask, something that would not become common until about a decade after this game in 1939.

The leading Houston High School scorer in 1917, guard Bennie Levison, is pictured above in this photograph. Below is center Warner Duckett, a junior who came to HHS from North Side Junior High School and scored 40 total points in six games to earn his own notoriety. Duckett was also the school's only pole vaulter, winning the event at meets at Rice and Texas A&M and capturing the Texas high school pole-vault title in 1917.

Pictured here is the 1924 girls' basketball team at Houston High School. The city had only one high school for years, and the names Houston, Sam Houston, and Central High were used somewhat interchangeably. Positions listed for the players that year were a forward, four guards, a jumping center, and two running centers.

The Jefferson Davis Panthers of 1930 finished 5-4, with an additional 4-1 record at a tournament in Huntsville. Basketball teams played a much shorter schedule back then. Davis faced the other four city schools twice each, plus Lufkin High School once. Players still jumped center after each basket, so scores were low. The Panthers' highest point total was 38 versus Milby, and the lowest scoring game was a 19-11 loss to Reagan High School.

Third-year coach Walter Hodges led the San Jacinto Bears to the city title in 1927–1928 in spite of the fact that he had only one returning letterman, team captain "Hokie" Snider. Hodges described his team as "small but fast with good eyes for the basket." Officially the team went 10-1 on the season, losing only to Beaumont 26-22, but that didn't include preseason tune-ups against opponents such as Southern Pacific Railroad.

After graduating from San Jacinto High School, Denton Cooley took his basketball talent to the University of Texas at Austin. He received a scholarship and, along with it, a section of the stands at Gregory Gym that he was told he needed to sweep out. Cooley dutifully handled the broom for about two weeks until he noticed none of the other players were doing any sweeping. (Dr. Denton A. Cooley.)

Denton A. Cooley scores on a layup at Madison Square Garden against Manhattan College in December 1939. The Longhorns took a road trip by train, stayed at the Hotel Piccadilly in New York, caught a Broadway show, and then beat the Jaspers 54-32. The crowd of more than 18,400 fans paid to see a college doubleheader, with the University of Southern California and Long Island University in the other matchup. (Dr. Denton A. Cooley.)

The Webster School had been around for a few decades, but the demographics changed when Seito Saibara, a wealthy lawyer from Kyoto, Japan, established a rice farm at Webster in 1903, bringing tenant farmers with him in the process. It proved to be one of the most successful cases of Japanese immigration to Texas, as the new Americans quickly became a valued part of the community, including important contributors to the basketball team. Here the team poses outdoors, underscoring the fact that many of the more rural county schools played basketball on very rudimentary courts that were completely open to the elements. (HMRC.)

The 1939–1940 boys' basketball team at Stephen F. Austin High School was not especially memorable for success on the court, but its players were enthusiastic. City high schoolers played home-and-home against the other Houston schools in the absence of a central field house.

Setting a new record for wins by a Houston team, the 1945 Milby Buffaloes went 32-1. Unfortunately the lone loss came at the hands of Fort Worth's Paschal High School in the state semifinals. The Buffaloes outscored district opponents 705-356, including a record-breaking 84-12 whipping of San Jacinto. Billy Joe Steakley was the top scorer, putting up 35 points in the San Jacinto game to best Slater Martin's city record. (Milby High School.)

The *Houston Post* reported on the morning of March 11, 1929, that Galena Park High School had won the Harris County basketball championships for both boys and girls. Coach W. H. Pond led the boys' team. Carroll Melton, the Yellow Jackets center (pictured here holding the ball), was a star of the team. He had scored 21 of the team's 27 points against La Porte High School earlier in the season. (HMRC.)

The San Jacinto High School tennis team of 1927–1928 had three star players: Winthrop Carter and Henry Holden (pictured third and fourth from left, respectively) and Lewis Brazelton (not pictured). The doubles teams of Holden and Brazelton and Carter and Brazelton each took titles, and Henry Holden won the city singles championship, for which he was awarded the cup he is holding.

In only the second year of its existence, the Lamar High School girls' tennis team won the city and district championships. From left to right, Nancy Nelms, Ann Wallis, and Agnese Nelms stand somberly in front of the net. Agnese later became best known for her staunch defense of accused communist spy Alger Hiss, with whom she had worked at the Carnegie Endowment for International Peace.

The San Jacinto High School girls' tennis team played not only on the courts but also on the stage. They combined with the boys' tennis team to raise money in 1928 that was used to pay off a debt for resurfacing and fencing the school tennis courts. The fund-raiser was a three-act production of *The Mystery of the Three Gables*, with the players acting the roles.

The Central High School Tigers swim team poses barefoot on the steps of the relatively new school in 1924. The old high school had burned in 1919 and was rebuilt on the same block at Rusk and Caroline Streets a year later. The building shown here was the third high school on the spot and later served as the Houston Independent School District administration building until being demolished for a parking lot in the 1970s.

The indoor swimming pool at Central High School downtown was not at all unusual in Houston. Most other city high schools and junior high schools also boasted indoor pools. Though girls wore swimsuits, boys often swam naked since wool fibers from the suits were believed to unduly clog the pool filters.

These 14 students posing on the diving board comprised the Jefferson Davis High School swim team in 1931. Four of them also served on the Life Savers, a group of five total who doubled as lifeguards. High schools occasionally let children from neighborhood grade schools use their pools.

The San Jacinto High School girls' swim team won the city championship by trouncing Davis High School 72-21 at a meet held at the YWCA. The stars were Amy Oliver (second from left, front row) and Valerie Calhoun (third from left, middle row). The silver cup in the photograph was the championship trophy donated by J J Sweeney Jewelers.

The girls of the pep squad at Jeff Davis High School on Quitman Street have formed a large letter "D" in the school gym in 1931. The gymnasium seating is all on a second level above the court. During basketball games, which were usually held on a home-and-home basis among Houston high schools, fans lined the catwalks on either side to observe the action on the hardwood from above.

The oversized sleeves on the uniform shirts of the 1940 Reagan High School cheerleaders make them look a bit like the Flying Wallendas, but it does nothing to diminish the spirit they had for the beloved Bulldogs of Houston Heights. Reagan High School opened in 1927, taking the place of Heights High School. The Bulldog mascot and school colors remained the same at the new location.

Houston High School's Black Battalion are setting a stylish standard as they parade here in the mid-1920s. The Black Battalion, later renamed the Tigerettes, was not merely the first girls' military drill team, it also claimed to be the first such entity in the nation. Clearly the squad wore black uniforms complete with capes, but its yearbook page also features a large photograph of the school principal, Frank M. Black.

Even faced with the rationing and other deprivations of the World War II home front, the Gauchos drill team from San Jacinto High School continued to rise to all challenges. The 1945 squad performed at all the school's football games in addition to making many civic appearances at events such as the Armistice Day Parade and the Shrine Ball.

Girls' volleyball was an intramural sport in 1927–1928, with various classes competing against one another. Ellen Wellensiek (holding the ball) was the captain and star player for the seventh-period team at San Jacinto High School. They defeated the girls' fourth-period team to win the school crown.

This 1938 gym class at Lamar High School seems to be having more fun than achieving gymnastic perfection. The school had a policy to attain health and happiness, noting "physical well being is essential for a happy life." It offered girls' volleyball, basketball, dancing, and posture training to make it so.

Ice hockey was considered a club sport at most high schools in 1934, but the players were competitive with sometimes older opponents, even if the team's goalie seems to be wearing a baseball catcher's chest protector.

Though the starter appears to have a pistol, the runners clearly have no starting blocks, the absence of which produces a variety of jumps for the sprinters. The track, smoothed for running, was in an unfenced area on the south side of the San Jacinto campus, possibly one of the many unpaved streets that Houston still had in 1928. Two gentlemen casually converse at the corner behind them. A year later, the Bears track team won the state championship.

Anthony Aucoin, a junior at San Jacinto High School, practices the high jump on the school athletic fields in 1928. The team did well, winning invitational meets at Rice Institute and at Texas A&M. The only competition it lost all season was when it traveled to East Texas for the Piney Woods meet.

These three San Jacinto High School hurdlers practice behind the school. The team won the city title in 1928 under first-year coach Cap Harding, repeating a feat they had accomplished the year prior. Showmanship was not unheard of in those days. Five years hence, hurdler Truman Thomas won bets by knocking a quarter from the high hurdles in full stride without ever disturbing the hurdle itself.

Five

KIDS

Girls have a turn at recess at a very basic Houston school playground in 1913. Though the dresses are different, everyone is wearing stockings, a requirement of modesty even for grammar school-age girls. The area behind the school yard appears to be quite rural, but it was developed enough to have a fire hydrant.

Girls and boys pose on the outdoor gym at Fannin School in 1911. Insurance companies would pale at this sort of recreation today. Fannin was a beautiful three-story brick school located at Louisiana and Tuam Streets. A few trees from the campus still remain.

Organized competition among grammar, or elementary, schools was a regular occurrence in the 1910s with the awarding of city championships being the rule in most sports. The Travis Elementary School track team from Woodland Heights stands before the banner they won in 1912.

The indoor baseball team at Austin School, located on St. Emanuel Street on the east side of downtown, won five consecutive city championships among the grammar schools. This 1911 squad poses in street clothes.

Calisthenics date back to ancient Greece when a Persian scout at Thermopylae reported that the Spartan warriors were weak because they were performing some sort of synchronized dance. Calisthenics were a staple for Houston schoolchildren for decades in the days before free weights and ubiquitous gym memberships.

H. G. Spruce, a graduate of the University of Chicago and Southwestern University, was in his first year as baseball coach at South End Junior High School in 1918. The yearbook gave an up-to-the-minute report that "Up to April 25 South End has played four games and lost one." The loss came via St. Thomas High School, and the vanquished foes included Harrisburg and Ball High School of Galveston.

Coach C. J. Sherman had charge of the South End boys' basketball team in 1918. Though only a ninth-grader, team captain Leonard Attwell was described as "one of the most feared men on the team." They are indeed a tough-looking bunch.

The girls of South End Junior High School in 1918 were fortunate that modern educators had awakened to the benefits of physical education. The school offered organized volleyball, basketball, and indoor baseball teams for the young ladies, with all three sporting the same uniforms. Misses Parsons and Winn were the coaches for the basketball team shown here.

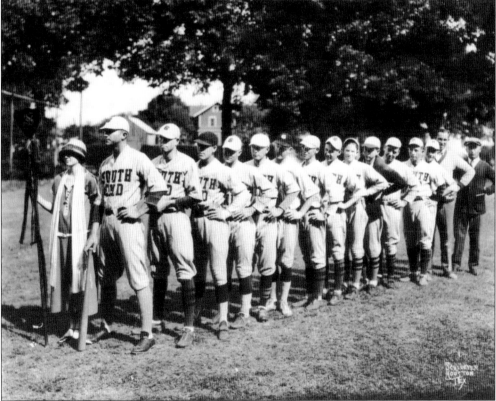

The baseball team at South End lines up behind the school talisman and their coach. It opened as one of the original junior highs in Houston, but in 1926, it was converted to a high school with the student body voting to change the name to San Jacinto, reportedly since many of their uniforms already had the letter "S." (HMRC.)

Kiddie Wonderland had rides, but the ponies were always the attraction. Many Houstonians had their first equine experience plodding around the track along Main Street on ponies with names like Smoky, Spanky, or Champ. One of the park's claims to fame was that actress Candace Bergen rode the ponies while her ventriloquist father was in town performing at the nearby Shamrock Hotel. (Geneva Carter.)

Kiddie Wonderland lasted almost 60 years on South Main Street between Braeswood Boulevard and Kirby Drive. At the time this photograph was taken in the 1940s, the area was considered the outskirts of town. The miniature train that circled the few acres started life in the late 1930s under steam power but was converted to gasoline. By the time the park closed, it had been inoperable for a few years. (Geneva Carter.)

The cap-wearing youngster steering the no. 97 locomotive in a perfect circle is Walter Carter Jr. of Houston Heights. Rides from the 1930s and earlier were repaired many times over the years, including a 1914 C. W. Parker carousel. The land was owned by the Ben Taub family, who leased it to the various tenants that ran the park on a year-to-year basis from 1936 until the last pony ride in 1994. By that time, grandparents were bringing grandchildren to enjoy the same rides that once thrilled them. (Geneva Carter.)

When O. D. Drain opened Kiddie Wonderland on six-plus acres of dusty prairie in 1936, it was a drive of a few miles back to where most of the city ended near Rice Institute. The rather small Ferris wheel was operated by hand, and it was incumbent upon the toddlers riding it to hang onto the safety bar. (Geneva Carter.)

One of the signature rides at Kiddie Wonderland was the collection of motorboats that graced the park for more than 50 years with only minor alterations. The boats were reminiscent of classic Chris Crafts but with multiple steering wheels so every kid could drive.

Twelve-year-old Billy Martin was the unquestioned star of the Houston team that won the Little League World Series on August 26, 1950. Martin had already thrown two no-hitters on the year, including one against Westerly, Rhode Island, just two days before. In the final game, Martin, throwing to battery mate Gerald Walling, allowed only a single and a walk while striking out 11 to beat Bridgeport, Connecticut, by a score of 2-1. The team's train was met two days later by a large welcoming celebration at Union Station, including music courtesy of the Ellington Field's Band. (Peter J. McGovern Little League Museum.)

Snowball fights are rare in Houston, but January 30, 1949, brought 2.6 inches of snow officially. The fourth most snow ever recorded in the city, it provided plenty of the white stuff in which to play. The King family gets ready to pelt the photographer in their yard in Idylwood. (Lesta King family.)

Playing tug of war in the front yard is a simple way to kill a summer afternoon for anyone still of the age that doesn't mind the Houston heat. These kids are in Woodlands Heights, but the scene could have happened in any of Houston's post–World War II neighborhoods.

Six

AIR AND WATER

Young William and Barbara Morris pose on the beach in Galveston with the pagoda of the Sui Jen Restaurant in the background. In 1935, the west end of the island was ranch land, so most beachgoers from Houston pitched their towels and umbrellas beneath the seawall. At the onset of World War II, the Japanese-themed Sui Jen became the Balinese Room. (Miriam Trost, William A. Morris Collection.)

Structures on the water have rarely stood up against the fury of Gulf hurricanes. The pier and bathhouses at Sylvan Beach were wrecked in the storm of 1900, but they were rebuilt along with these diving platforms soon afterward. A dip in the bay was an extremely popular way to cool off, even in wool bathing suits. These would be destroyed again in August 1915. (HMRC.)

The annual Houston Bathing Girl Revue started at Sylvan Beach in La Porte in 1924. Scantily clad contestants who represented businesses from around the county drew the biggest crowds of the season. Spectators came by car, train, or excursion boats from the Harrisburg dock to cheer the girls. A Sylvan Beach park manager reported that many of the girls later married the businessmen who sponsored them. (Bay Area Historical Society.)

The bayside retreat of Sylvan Beach opened in the 1890s, and though its heyday would come after World War I, it was still a destination in 1914. A railroad depot was opened at the park's land entrance that year, and the "Moonlight Excursion" train left Houston at 7 p.m. and returned at midnight. The rare grove of trees made a prime spot for picnics, fishing, and enjoying music and dancing on the open-air floor. (HMRC.)

Bathhouses like Murdoch's offered Galveston beachgoers a place to change plus dining with a Gulf view, souvenirs, and photograph booths with faux oceanside backgrounds. The high-water mark for Galveston's bathhouses was in the years before and after World War I, but Murdoch's still flourished here in 1935. (Miriam Trost, William A. Morris Collection.)

The German population in Houston has been substantial since the 1840s, and several German activity societies were staples of the city's social life. In 1923, a group broke away from the established Saengerbund to start a new German singing club called the Liederkranz, which had a clubhouse at Barnes and Abbott Streets. One early outing took members to an area swimming hole for a picnic and a dip. (Susan Schulz.)

Since the earliest days of Houston, boys counted on Buffalo Bayou for recreation. Swimming holes known as "the Sycamores," at the foot of Smith Street, and "the Arsenal," at the foot of LaBranch Street, were among the early favorites. As the 20th century unfolded, popular swimming holes moved outward to places like Shepherd's Dam or the Schneider Place on White Oak Bayou. Bathing suits were not a known commodity. (UHSC.)

Vick's Lake was a popular destination on Buffalo Bayou in the years before World War I. The Vick family home sat on the north bank of the bayou on land where they had once grazed cattle, and residents from Houston Heights often came down the Boulevard to swim, picnic, or canoe in the nearby lake that bore the family's name. Eventually the area became a city park in 1917. The lake was described as a small oxbow shape that was filled in during the construction of the Waugh Drive and Memorial cloverleaf. A small portion of what was once 44 acres of parkland still remains in Spotts Park. (UHSC.)

In 1942, when these kids were splashing about the pool at Linder Lake, it was one of a handful available to Houston's general public. The city operated three segregated swimming pools: Stude Park and Mason Park for whites and Emancipation Park for African Americans, all at the cost of a dime or a quarter. The Heights Natatorium was also open for white swimmers. Linder Lake Pool was a north-side hangout from the 1930s to 1960s. (Miriam Trost, William A. Morris Collection.)

Like many other Houstonians, William A. and Ollie Morris were regulars at Magnolia Gardens, a long-lived swimming and concert venue on the San Jacinto River near Sheldon. Located on a sweeping bend north of the Highway 90 bridge, the river supplied Magnolia Gardens with a wide sand beach. Among the many music acts that played there in the years after this 1946 photograph was a young unknown named Elvis Presley. (Miriam Trost, William A. Morris Collection.)

The best aquatic stars in the South converged on the Houston Country Club pool for an August weekend event in 1928. New Orleanian Buddy Smith was the star of the annual Southern Amateur Athletic Union meet, winning by breaking his own records at 50 and 220 yards and also winning at 100 and 440 yards. The meet was moved from the Heights Natatorium, because divers required 10 feet of water under the board. The club from the Heights Natatorium was the most successful of the local swimmers, however, with winning performances from Bob Waite in the 100-yard breast stroke, D. W. Humason in the back stroke, and Lillian Shepherd in the 50-yard dash. (HMRC.)

Large boats such as the *Nicholaus*, based out of the Harrisburg docks, ferried people from Houston to events down the bayou. The docks were located at the foot of Market Street in the heart of old Harrisburg, where Braes Bayou emptied into Buffalo. Thousands of people journeyed to the San Jacinto Battleground to picnic and watch the festivities. (HMRC.)

The *Houston Post* of April 21, 1920, stated that the crowd at that day's San Jacinto celebration would "eclipse anything of the kind ever attempted in South Texas." Thousands packed lunches and migrated to the battleground park to watch athletic competitions, an airplane circus, and a greasy pole-climbing event in which anyone reaching the top without assistance received $5.

Family and friends of Dan E. Kennedy gather at his Morgan's Point house for the launch of the sailboat *Ethylwayne*. Kennedy, in the bowler hat, was a former Texas Ranger and the son of early Houston merchant John Kennedy. He was named the first commodore of the new Houston Yacht Club in February 1898. (Houston Yacht Club Archives, Humphreville-Beasley Collection.)

William E. Humphreville, a local brick and cement contractor, built the *Hudie* at his home at 1803 Leeland Street in 1906. When the boat was finished, it was hauled down Main Street for launching into Buffalo Bayou. The South Texas Grain Company on Willow Street is visible across the bayou. Humphreville would later serve as commodore of the Houston Yacht Club. (Houston Yacht Club Archives, Humphreville-Beasley Collection.)

When the Houston Yacht Club was first organized, it maintained a dock at the foot of Travis Street. In 1910, the club, sometimes known as the Houston Launch Club, moved to Harrisburg to a more central bayou location on the south side of a channel that ran behind Brady Island. Yacht club members at that time owned an amazing array of motorized pleasure craft that were ideally suited to getting the most out of life on the water. These yachts were ideal for entertaining and for mitigating the Houston heat with some gentle breezes off the water. (Above, Houston Yacht Club Archives, Baker Collection.)

Home of the Houston Launch Club, Houston, Texas

Harry Baker was an active member of the Houston Yacht Club for the early decades of its existence. He often piloted this boat, named for U.S. senator Joe Bailey, the type of powerboat that was extremely popular among club members who had a need for speed when enjoying the many rustic sections of Buffalo Bayou around 1910. (Houston Yacht Club Archives, Baker Collection.)

Two electric-powered launches, with the one in the foreground flying the burgee of the Houston Yacht Club, ply Buffalo Bayou around 1906. Elco, the Electric Launch Company, debuted the launches at the World's Columbian Exposition of 1893, with 55 of the boats ferrying passengers around the exposition's watercourses. They remained quite popular through the turn of the century in both America and Europe before oil-powered motors cornered the market. (Houston Yacht Club Archives.)

When the Houston Yacht Club, the oldest such organization in Texas, started in 1897, it was based downtown, but most of its regattas took place off Seabrook or Sylvan Beach. This is most likely a postcard image of its regatta in August 1902. (Houston Yacht Club Archives.)

A race of Corinthian-class sloops starts at the judges' stand off Shoreacres. The Texas Corinthian Yacht Club, formed by Houston Yacht Club members in 1938, commissioned the New York firm of Sparkman and Stephens to design a boat specifically suited to Galveston Bay's strong winds and shallow depths. The resulting 21-foot boats were a staple of bay sailing through the 1970s. (Houston Yacht Club Archives, Billy Moody Collection.)

In the years between the two world wars, the Houston Yacht Club joined yacht clubs around the Gulf to compete for the Lipton Cup, a silver trophy donated by a world-famous British sailor and tea magnate. All competitors sailed 20-foot, gaff-rigged sloops of one design, called "fish boats." The yachting press dubbed Houston the team to beat in 1928, when the meet was held off New Orleans. Five local sailors, led by George Humphreville, made the trip to the Crescent City, but the team fell short of bringing home the trophy. The Houston Yacht Club never won the Lipton Cup, but it did host the regatta twice, in 1929 and again in 1941. (Houston Yacht Club Archives, Hamilton Collection.)

Mayor H. Baldwin Rice's 90-foot yacht, *Zeeland*, was often used to promote the Houston Ship Channel, but Rice also loaned it to friends. In 1907, Houston buggy dealer Edwin Larendon was the sole passenger on a relaxing cruise through the Great Lakes and down the Mississippi River when the *Zeeland* was attacked by locals at a small Illinois town who were upset with other yachtsmen for coming ashore to woo their women. (UHSC.)

Four Chris Craft runabouts with triple cockpits race near the Houston Yacht Club around 1932. *Angelina*, the boat in the foreground, was owned by Willis Goodman, who also happened to be a local Chris Craft dealer. Second in line is *Butterkrust*, named after the bread sold by the family of boat owner H. J. Schott. (Houston Yacht Club Archives.)

Men are seen posing around a lightweight Bleriot airplane at a show staged by Moisant's International Aviators in January 1911. Siblings John, Alfred, and Matilde—the latter being the second American woman to become a licensed pilot—barnstormed through the United States, Mexico, and Cuba with other top fliers during those two years, reportedly earning more than $100,000 each. The most famous Moisant brother, John, had learned to fly in France from Louis Bleriot himself and was the first to carry a passenger from Paris to London. He was the owner of a modified Bleriot monoplane, which he dubbed the *Statue of Liberty*, the first single-wing aircraft to fly in the United States. One month before the Houston meet, John Moisant was killed in a plane crash at Kenner outside of New Orleans. The municipal airport, still located in that suburb, was named in his honor. (UHSC.)

Crowds of up to 8,000 were drawn to air meets to witness new technology firsthand. One of the highlights of the Moisant air show held on the prairie near Bellaire was a flight by French aviator Roland Garros, who soared to 5,000 feet, dancing in and out of the clouds and disappearing from view for a full five minutes before cutting his motor and gliding low over the top of the stands to a perfect landing in the center of the field. (UHSC.)

The weeklong aviation meet in January 1911 was held on the prairie at Westmoreland Farms near the new town of Bellaire. The partially assembled aeroplanes arrived by train and created quite a stir as they passed through town. Special streetcars and trains took passengers to the aviation grounds, where they paid 50¢ for general admission or $1.50 for box seats. Parking for cars was $1. (UHSC.)

S. E. J. Cox, whose name appears on the plane in the background, was an oilman and millionaire sportsman. The three wearing flight gear are Cox, his wife, and their son Seymour, all of whom were flyers. Mrs. Cox once flew from Houston to New York to take young Seymour to school. In 1920, a year after this photograph was taken, Cox claimed his *Texas Wildcat* had shattered the world's airspeed record with a mark of 223 miles per hour. He offered to spend $100,000 that year to win the coveted James Gordon Bennett Trophy for the Aero Club of Texas. In 1922, while Cox was racing his airplanes, he was indicted in Houston on charges that he defrauded investors in several of his oil and land companies. (UHSC.)

Charles K. Hamilton was one of America's best-known aviators after he became the first to fly round-trip between New York and Philadelphia in June 1910; he made the first-ever night flight just weeks later. He took part in the Houston air meet of January 1911, showcasing his black biplane, the *Hamiltonian*, which featured a 14-cylinder, 110-horsepower Gnome motor. In 1913, he returned to the area for exhibitions such as racing this automobile along the beach at Galveston, a popular stunt of the day. (Library of Congress.)

Fifteen entrants left Houston Speedway on July 4, 1930, as part of the National Balloon Race for one of three U.S. spots in the international Gordon Bennett balloon race. The National Balloon Race was won by the Goodyear-Zeppelin team of R. J. Blair, a former navy yard riveter, and 29-year-old aeronautics student Frank Trotter, who made it almost 800 miles to near Greeensburg, Kentucky. Thunderstorms forced 10 of the 15 balloons to land, and others jettisoned contents. (Sloane Collection.)

Seven

ROD AND GUN

E. A. "Squatty" Lyons, who served parts of five decades as a Harris County commissioner, catches a little sleep while fishing. Lyons's family owned a prominent store in Houston Heights. Once in a room full of East Coast businessmen, he calmly noted that he graduated from Harvard, without mentioning it was the Heights elementary school. (Lyons family.)

James Mohle, Jim Hulme, and Woodrow "Frog" Todd were fishing buddies who often made a trip to South Texas or Mexico, because that was where to find the biggest fish. They and a helper are loading a grouper into a chest freezer in Hulme's pickup, which advertises his new appliance business on Shepherd Drive near Washington Avenue. He said it was "the only business he could start with a rusty screwdriver and a pair of pliers." (Anne Sloan.)

This day's catch was a good one, but the prize is clearly the tarpon. Anyone wanting to fish offshore in 1914 likely had to rely on one of a few charter boats, since almost no sportfishermen owned Gulf-worthy boats. Tarpon, though, were so plentiful in the Galveston Bay system that they could be caught from the surf at the beach or as far up the bay as where Interstate 10 crosses the San Jacinto River today. (HMRC.)

Though bait camps did exist on Galveston Island in later years, at places like Della's at the base of the causeway, M&M on Offat's Bayou, or a collection of camps at the east end of the seawall, most people in 1910 wouldn't have dreamt of buying bait. A few casts of a net would yield all the bait one needed. If shrimp were wanted for dinner, the same net could save a person the cost of 10¢ per pound. (Moody family/Doug McLeod.)

Heald Bank, about 34 miles east of Galveston, remains a popular offshore fishing spot today. At the time this bounty of fish was caught, the water depth of about 30 feet was marked with a red-hulled lightship bearing two lanterns. Reliable boat motors had expanded the range for fisherman over what it was in earlier years. These men may have been a random group aboard a charter boat. (HMRC.)

Several boys and one intrepid woman fish from Shepherd's Dam on Buffalo Bayou as several others enjoy the view from the bridge in the background. Shepherd's Dam Road was the early name for today's Shepherd Drive. The iron and wood bridge spanned the bayou from the 1890s until 1922. Memoirs from the era say that this spot was teeming with black bass. (UHSC.)

From left to right, Kathleen, Florine, and Albert Kleb Jr. pose on the porch of their Houston Heights home with kingfish caught by their father in 1940. A. B. Kleb Sr. regularly went fishing off Freeport in a 16-foot boat that he helped build at the Telge Top and Body Works on Heights Boulevard near Center Street. (A. B. Kleb.)

Galveston businessman W. L. Moody Jr. loved fishing and hunting more than almost anything and spent a lifetime enjoying the outdoors. A widower by 1948, Moody thought that this fishing picture would make a dandy Christmas card, something that his wife would have never allowed. (Moody family/Doug McLeod.)

Leonard Schwab and his children (from left to right) Bob, Marcia, and Pat, spend a day fishing at the Texas City Dike. The dike, protruding about five miles into Galveston Bay, was built in the mid-1910s as a breakwater to keep silt out of the Texas City Channel. (Pat Schwab.)

Most hunters simply approached a farmer and asked permission to hunt, even for overnight stays, but local boys were available as guides, just in case, for about $3 a gun. For bird hunters in Houston, choices were many. The bay promised an abundance of waterfowl almost beyond imagination, and open prairies could be found to the east, west, or south. (HMRC.)

Ella Kleb might not have been the one who did the actual wild turkey hunting, but she donned her husband's gear when he returned from the hunt and struck a serious pose in front of the family home on Tulane Street in Houston Heights in the 1920s. (A. B. Kleb.)

W. L. Moody Jr. poses after a successful duck hunt at his ranch at Smith Point in 1947. The birds were so numerous in the late 19th century—before pollution and ship traffic destroyed most of Galveston Bay's oyster beds and vegetation—that Moody's father was among those running a market duck business on their land. Dressed ducks were loaded in barrels and taken by boat back to Galveston, where they were shipped to the East. (Moody family/Doug McLeod.)

Joseph Watkins Elsbury (left) and his brother-in-law John Emmet Price, known as "Pike," shot these ducks just beyond Sugar Land in 1917. They noted, "All Mallards except 2–3 canvasbacks." Both men enlisted in the U.S. Army later that year. After serving, they returned to Houston to a big family house on Rosalie Street and jobs in the oil business. Elsbury continued to be an avid duck hunter, too. (Kathy Riedel Davis.)

Four natives of Rose Hill who had moved to Houston Heights return from a duck hunt in 1940. With a pass issued by the Freeport Sulphur Company, which owned the land, they had a very successful day on the prairies at Hoskins Mound near what is today the Brazoria National Wildlife Refuge. It is an area that sits at the end of the central migratory flyway with freshwater sloughs winding through saltwater marshes. Hunting for ducks and geese is still allowed in an area on Christmas Point. (A. B. Kleb.)

If a hunter wanted to bring back a trophy buck, the place to buy sporting goods was at C. L. Bering's. That was the message inherent in the frequent displays of local hunters and fishermen photographed in front of the downtown store with their quarry. Most sporting goods stores used professional photographers for the purpose. (HMRC.)

The Lyons Feed Store on Washington Avenue sold groceries and lunches. There is no record of who was treated to venison after this 1938 hunt, but E. A. "Squatty" Lyons (right) shows off two bucks in a time-honored Texas fashion before they met their destiny of sausage, chili, and trophies. (Lyons family.)

In sheer numbers, there might be a larger whitetail deer population in Texas now than 100 years ago, but the hunting pressure was much lighter. The limit on deer around the turn of the last century was six bucks during the two-month deer season. They were hunted in woods around the Houston area, but some serious hunters rode the train to a hill country destination seeking bigger animals. (HMRC.)

A. B. Kleb Jr. doesn't see eye to eye with a buck he shot from a tree on his family's property near Spring Creek and Mueschke Road. The Klebs had been hunting that tract since they bought the property in the 1920s, more than 40 years after the first family members settled in northwest Harris County. (A. B. Kleb.)

Billed as "the Wonderful Topperweins,"—a slightly Americanized spelling of their last name, Toepperwein—San Antonio residents "Ad" and "Plinky" were national stars. Adolph, previously performing as a single in vaudeville and with a circus, was billed as the "World's Greatest Rifle Shot." His wife gained fame trap shooting with a shotgun, once setting a world endurance record by shooting 1,952 out of 2,000 targets in five hours and 20 minutes. She also came to Houston as a competitive bowler. (Robert P. Cochran.)

From their first appearance at the St. Louis World's Fair of 1904 until her death in 1945, Adolph "Ad" and Elizabeth "Plinky" Toepperwein were the most celebrated exhibition shooting act in America. Ad, a native of Leon Springs, Texas, was the son of a gunsmith and an accomplished shooter by age 10. He met Elizabeth while she was working at the Winchester Arms Company as an inspector, eventually marrying her and bringing her back to Texas. Behind them is signage for Plinky's sponsor, Dead Shot Powder, which advertised that bird hunters could expect "lightning-like rapidity, the closest pattern and the lightest recoil." (Robert P. Cochran.)

Plinky Toepperwein was not only one of the most popular shooters at the annual Sunny South Handicap, but she was also among the most successful. In 1909, she won a $100 prize, paid in gold pieces, and was accompanied to a show at the Prince Theatre downtown by several in the otherwise all-male field. Shortly thereafter, Buffalo Bill Cody presented her with the Native American–made, beaded ammunition pouch that she is wearing here in 1912. (Robert P. Cochran.)

Dead Shot Powder was one of several shooting products that loved to advertise at events like the Sunny South Handicap. The six-day-long shooting competition moved from Brenham to Houston in 1909. One of the regular winners in those early years was Houston businessman Otto Sens, who not only hit 185 out of 200 targets as an amateur in 1909, he also bought the Houston Buffs baseball club that year. (Robert P. Cochran.)

One of the most crowd-pleasing shooting stunts performed by Ad Toepperwein at his shows in Houston and elsewhere was his freehand drawing of a Native American head. He created the artwork with a .22 rifle manufactured by Winchester, the company for which he worked by touring the nation putting on exhibitions. (Robert P. Cochran.)

The Toepperweins' shows were a hit in Houston and smaller towns. Plinky not only shot shells off her husband's fingers, the pair also shot while standing on their heads, broke five clay pigeons sent aloft at once, hit targets from a speeding car, and shot cleanly through the middle of washers thrown into the air. One of Ad's best tricks was shooting a target thrown in front and one thrown behind him with simultaneous shots. (Robert P. Cochran.)

The State of Texas established the Fish and Oyster Commission to regulate overfishing in 1895 and added game to their purview 12 years later. That year they imposed a limit of 25 ducks, geese, or waterfowl per day. The first hunting licenses soon followed in 1909. (HMRC.)

ABOUT THE
ORGANIZATION

Houston Arts and Media's (HAM) mission is simple. We help filmmakers, screenwriters, authors, and other local talent create better and more innovative ways to teach both children and adults about history, science, literature, and the world. HAM has spent the last several years concentrating on projects for video, print, and Web delivery that involve state and local history. Our vision is far ranging and imaginative. Above all, we want to put Houston's creative talents to work in ways that help others learn. We hope you will join and support HAM's efforts to make Houston's future, and its past, a little brighter. (Houston Arts and Media is a 501c3 tax exempt organization.)
www.houstonartsandmedia.org

—Mike Vance, executive director

www.arcadiapublishing.com

Discover books about the town where you grew up, the cities where your friends and families live, the town where your parents met, or even that retirement spot you've been dreaming about. Our Web site provides history lovers with exclusive deals, advanced notification about new titles, e-mail alerts of author events, and much more.

MADE IN THE USA

Arcadia Publishing, the leading local history publisher in the United States, is committed to making history accessible and meaningful through publishing books that celebrate and preserve the heritage of America's people and places. Consistent with our mission to preserve history on a local level, this book was printed in South Carolina on American-made paper and manufactured entirely in the United States.

This book carries the accredited Forest Stewardship Council (FSC) label and is printed on 100 percent FSC-certified paper. Products carrying the FSC label are independently certified to assure consumers that they come from forests that are managed to meet the social, economic, and ecological needs of present and future generations.

FSC
Mixed Sources
Product group from well-managed forests and other controlled sources

Cert no. SW-COC-001530
www.fsc.org
© 1996 Forest Stewardship Council

Find Your Place in History.